The Salad Bowl

*This book is dedicated to
John Walton Spencer Number 16 School,
my amazing son Mush and my
"know it all" nephew Arthur Delgado III.
Thank you all for the inspiration
to write a story so close to my heart.*

This is a work of fiction. Names, characters, places, and incidents either are the product of the author's imagination or used fictitiously. Any resemblance to actual persons living or dead, events, or locales is entirely coincidental.

Copyright © 2018 by Shenek S. Byrd
Illustrations by James Cotterman
All rights reserved.
No part of this book may be reproduced or used in any manner without
written permission of copyright owner except for the use of quotations in book review.
First paperback edition October 2018
ISBN 978-0-578-40328-1
Published by Tocsin Magazine
www.Tocsinmag.com

The Salad Bowl

Shanique Byrd

*First and foremost,
would like to thank each and every one of you for reading
"The Salad Bowl".*

I would also love to hear about your **Salad Bowl Challenge**.
To enter, simply have each student discuss when their family migrated to their current city or America. Then create your very own salad bowl using fruits, vegetables, etc.
Take a picture of your Salad Bowl, along with the name of your creation.
then email it to
Challenge@TheSaladBowlBook.com
Selected winners will receive a pizza party courtesy of Tocsin Magazine.

The First Day of School

Excitement and anxiety fill the air as fifth grade students nervously search for direction.

Those nervous students soon find comfort as they notice a tall slender teacher with a welcoming smile and friendly wave.

"Hello class, my name is Mrs. Mohamed. I would like to welcome you to the first day of class. I have placed a group exercise on each of your desks."

Mrs. Mohamed then points to a student,

"Hi, Lee, would you like to go first?"

"Yes, My name is Lee Wong and I've attended Sixteen School since the third grade. My family moved to America when I was 3 years old from China."

Mrs. Mohamed points to another student.

"Hi, my name is Sarah Nowak and I am new to Sixteen School. My great grandparents are from Poland. They came to America when my grandmother was a young girl."

"Hello everyone, my name is Jason Brown and I am a returning student. My dad, Ron, is from Jamaica; he came to America when he was my age. Who wants to go next? Melissa, I think you should go next."

"Thanks Jason, My name is Melissa Speranza and I've been a student at Sixteen School since Kindergarten. I think my grandparents came to America from Italy in 1930. Can I pick someone?"

"Sure," Mrs. Mohamed replies. "Arthur you're the lucky winner," Melissa asserts.

"Arthur is my best friend. We have been in the same class since Kindergarten." Melissa points at Arthur

"My name is Arthur Delgado and my grandparents are from Mexico. They came to America when my mother was 16 years old. Oh yea, I am a returning student too, but, I think you all know that because of Melissa's big mouth."

The students all laugh in unison.

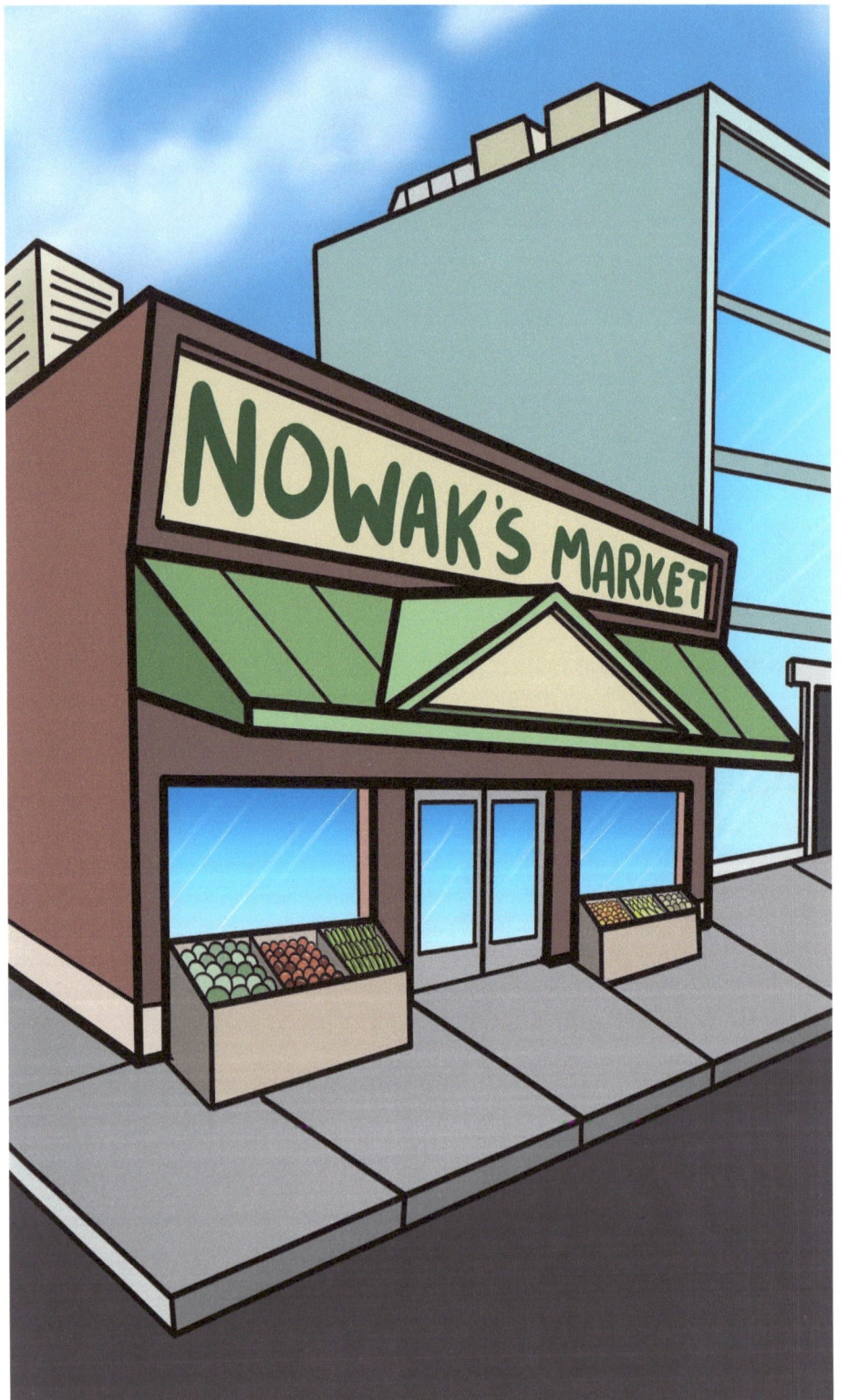

The bell rings, then Mrs. Mohamed announces to the class. "Tomorrow morning please bring a fruit or vegetable to class. You can pick something up from Nowak's Market on Main Street."

Sarah interrupts, "Nowak's Market? That's my parents' Market."

Arthur smiles, "My mom works there."

Lee jumps in, "My dad worked on that building!"

Jason yells, "My dad delivers milk and vegetables there!"

Melissa laughs, "My mom was the broker that helped the Nowaks find their building."

Mrs. Mohamed replies, "This is really exciting; I shop at Nowak's Market every Sunday. I love their vegetables. See, we are all connected in some small way."

Jason screams, "We're not done!"

Mrs. Mohamed looks confused, "What do you mean Jason?"

Jason smiles, " When did your family come to America?"

Mrs Mohamed laughs, "My family came to America eight years ago. My husband and I are from Iran. I've been teaching at Sixteen School for 3 years."

The following morning, the students notice a large bowl on the front of Mrs. Mohamed's desk, but she is nowhere in sight.

Jason says, "I didn't bring a fruit or vegetable, I brought in peanuts."

Melissa replies, "Peanuts, I think peanuts are a fruit, NOT," laughing "I brought in a tomato."

Arthur, "I brought in lettuce".

Lee smiles, "I brought in carrots!"

Sarah laughs, "I brought in carrots too."
As the students discuss what they brought in, Mrs. Mohamed walks in late.

"Mrs. Mohamed, I thought you weren't coming in today," Jason jokes.

"What do you think would happen if I didn't come in?" Mrs. Mohamed replies.
"We couldn't learn anything today, if you chose not to come in."

Mrs. Mohamed replies, "Correct, what would happen if none of you came in today?"

Arthur responds, "You couldn't teach anyone today if no one showed up."

Mrs. Mohamed affirms, "Exactly, now I want everyone to bring their vegetables and fruits up to my desk and place them in this bowl."

The students create a line and one by one, they place their items in the bowl.

Mrs. Mohamed looks around, "Did everyone put something in the bowl?"

The students all reply yes.

Mrs. Mohamed looks in the bowl, then says,

"We have nuts, carrots, lettuces, tomatoes, broccoli, cucumbers, an apple and a few other items."

"I think we should give it a name," Melissa blurts out.

"Melissa, that's a wonderful idea. Class, what should we call our mixture?" Mrs. Mohamed asks.

Sarah shouts, "The Community Salad!"

"Let's call it 'Hope Salad'," Arthur replies.

"Great, we will call it the "Community Hope Salad." Mrs. Mohamed determines."

"Nice…." Melissa smiles.

"Do we have to eat what's in the bowl?" Lee asks.

Mrs. Mohamed laughs, "No, but we do have to mentally eat what's in the bowl. Could anyone tell me the reason behind our salad bowl?"

Sarah queries, "So we can learn how to share?"

"The bowl symbolizes America and the items we placed in it represent us, the Americans that make up this country. We all bring our own flavor to this great land that we call home. The Nowak's Market is a great example of how our community works together to help it to function successfully. Without one person, our job would be a lot harder, sometimes even impossible, as you all have learned." Mrs. Mohamed states.

Arthur yells, "Are we the apples, tomatoes, and carrots of our Community Hope Salad?"

"Yes and so much more," Mrs. Mohamed replies

www.ingramcontent.com/pod-product-compliance
Lightning Source LLC
Chambersburg PA
CBHW041744040426
42444CB00001B/30